New American People

Enrico Natali

New American People

With an Introduction by Hugh Edwards

A Morgan & Morgan Monograph

©Enrico Natali 1972

Morgan & Morgan, Inc., Publishers
400 Warburton Avenue
Hastings-on-Hudson, N.Y. 10706

International Standard Book
Number ISBN 0-87100-023-7

Library of Congress
Catalog Card No. 79-188166

Designed by Rostislav Eismont
Typography by Typographic
Innovations, Inc.
Printing by Rapoport Printing
Company
Binding by A. Horowitz & Son

Printed in U.S.A.

Acknowledgment is made to
Alfred A. Knopf, Inc., for permission
to quote from Jacques Ellul's
A Critique of the New Commonplaces,
translated from the French by Helen Weaver,
copyright 1968 by Alfred A. Knopf, Inc.

For Gale and Vincenzo

Introduction

There are as many kinds of realism as there are of truth, and these photographs by Enrico Natali may have interpretations as various as the individuals who look at them. This would indicate they do not dictate messages, but provoke responses, a welcome feature in the midst of the babel of statements of problems, solutions and attitudes by which we find ourselves confused. They are gratifying, also, because they do not exaggerate, underestimate, or try to persuade. One is left face to face with them, alone, and free to develop any opinion to which they may give rise. Each of them is an entity, but together they create the illusion of a completeness that extends far beyond the selection in the book.

Indeed, they need no commentary, and the pictures that follow will easily efface these remarks. Many regard writing about photography as superfluous, and claim that little of it has any value. Perhaps this is due to photography itself which should be revelation enough both of content and of those who are trying to project it. Two of the usual criticisms of what is written concerning it are that this literature is too often directed to the public, and that it does not limit itself strictly to photography. But what reason is there for stating anything, if not for the public, and as for digressions, should a masterpiece like the Essays of Montaigne, where they create form and substance, be banned because of them? Long ago, Vauvenargues said

there are people who read only to find faults. Perhaps the best appreciation or criticism of any work would be a mere description of it, so that the work would speak for itself without the interference of ideas outside it, and impression and judgment would be left to the viewer, reader or listener. But rare are those nowadays who are able to approach any achievement with freshness and innocence of estimate, free from the prejudices produced by what they have heard or read about it.

All the photographs in the present collection were taken in 1967-1970 in Detroit, which in no way restricts their presentation as a brief of how Americans look and live today. These scenes and incidents might have occurred anywhere in the United States in this time when regional characteristics are disappearing and it is difficult to select what is typical or isolate details which are significant. It does not matter that all who appear here are city dwellers. The distant rural areas, the small towns and larger metropolises are all suggested in these faces which reflect the standardizations of technocracy and modern democracy: this is a view of a situation and condition, not a localization. One of Enrico Natali's principal talents is an ability to detect the personal and unique which still manage to exist within the most commonplace settings and happenings, and over all the American character is prevalent. You could not find people like these anywhere else, and even the very atmosphere is present and felt as we who live here know it. So, as a whole, the collection is a valuable memoir which reveals more than a documentary: it is a representation of those quiet and undisturbed moments which may expose more of human beings and their dissimilarities than the abnormalities of upheaval and distress.

In 1967, during the months of convalescence from an accident in Arizona, Natali surveyed the accumulation of his negatives from about seven years of work. Much of this had been done on a variety of jobs, and the rest had been produced independently. Together they showed a certain consistency and logical coherence which were common both to assignments and independent work. With this was the gratifying discovery that there had begun to take shape a sizeable portrait of a large part of the American population which was being overlooked or intentionally disregarded. It was a time when poverty, violence, and sensationalism had usurped the stage, and the large majority had been relegated to a vast penumbra from which they were only occasionally recalled for intervals of satire or ridicule, then banished again to the immense half darkness. A new propaganda ruled, and the established pyramids had been placed on their apexes, surrounded by a cacophony of loud dogmas, nervous intellectuality, and stimulated chaos.

Esthetes and purists had mostly retired to academic shelters and were working to find new aspects and extensions of the medium. A tremendous production of photography was one result of these varied endeavors which ranged from bare documentation to rarefied estheticism; and finally, the survivors from all of it have been the works of certain talents which could outlive the excitement which motivated their first appearances.

Natali returned to Detroit and continued working. In the spring of 1969 an extensive exhibition of his photographs was shown at The Art Institute of Chicago where they faced a large and heterogeneous public, including many others than those for whom photography is a particular interest. The popularity of this show, which it had been supposed might meet with controversy, indifference, or opposition, required its two-month exhibition period to be extended.

Perhaps people enjoyed seeing themselves and their contemporaries without having to look through the barriers of interpretation or condescension, and they could be forgiven the mistake of conveniently labelling what they saw as a view of the new middle class. Even two years ago this had become an anachronism, and the words "middle class" and "bourgeois" had descended from their original meanings through the disparaging and pejorative to describe almost anything and anybody. The people in Natali's photographs are not situated on common economic or social levels: they are as if suspended in an ambience larger than any social classification which might attempt to categorize them. What we are beginning to realize at last is that the average way of life in present-day society is not merely keeping up with others and subscribing to social prejudices, establishments and organizations, but the spread of a kind of evolutionary force as irresistible and inevitable as what were called destiny and divine power, and against which man can make little effective resistance. Even revolution, as its reward, can offer no more than the benefits of this expanding condition, fortified by the wonders of technology, the ubiquity of information and knowledge, and the promise of an illusion of security. For the poor do not want to remain poor, and although a very wealthy society still persists in practicing a kind of life that now seems almost eccentric, both poor and rich are succumbing to the great levelling process. It may not be the way of happiness for exceptions, differences, misfits and variations, but it can contain them. It would surprise Whitman, who dreamed of the excellence of the average, and confirm Tocqueville, whose visionary intelligence foresaw the perils of the dictatorship of the majority and what we call fascism, which are its most dangerous potentialities.

Jacques Ellul, in *A Critique of the New Commonplaces,* has written a description of the modern predicament which could serve as an epigraph for this book of pictures: *Marxism is mistaken in believing that diffusion begins with the ruling class, for our civilization has become much more totalitarian than it was a century ago, and all men are involved in a process of common evolution. They belong to the development of the technological world before they belong to a class; they are people who share the atomic and demographic risk before they are a socialistic or capitalistic people; they belong to work and happiness before they are rich or poor. Our world has become one in its works and expressions, and this unity far exceeds all division, even those as serious as class or nation. This is why all people express themselves in the same way, all secrete the same values, and all have their eyes fixed on the same ideals. An admirable unity emerges that reveals the most ironic destiny.*

Natali presents a visual abstract of this vast subject without the condiments of new prejudices or the insinuations of interpretations, and although humor may be present, it never has the flavor of satire. He neither defends nor attacks, nor is there the slightest relinquishment of an inherent respect for his material. He understands fully the worth of those areas that exist between the photographer, the camera, and the subject, and one enjoys the grateful absence of self-expression.

This latter quality has been highly commended and encouraged in an era when art is too often prized for therapeutic and other compensatory or materialistic virtues which are actually no part of it. We have a surfeit of public catharses and there is a fashionable taste for monstrosities, freaks, and attempts to shock an unshockable age. Homer, Shakespeare, Balzac, Stendhal, Flaubert, James, Brancusi, and most artists who are remembered, were not striving to portray themselves, and yet their personal characters and individualities show through their works with a transparency far more revealing than if it were the principal aim: they identify themselves freely and surpass those who have made intentional confessions and self-revelations.

There is no better way to identity than objectivity without detachment, and we have a clear example in the following selection of photographs. That Natali's work developed autonomously, engendered only by personal conscientiousness and strict self-discipline, and that the direction it had taken became evident to him only later, are enough to give it merit and distinction. It is, however, the difference of viewpoint which strikes one when looking at these photographs the first time, and which sets them apart from so much that is being done today. In the last year there have been occasional appearances of outlook which have some relationship with them: Larry McMurtry's novel, *Moving On,* and Robert Rafelson's motion picture, *Five Easy Pieces,* did not suggest attitudes or offer solutions, and left the latter—if they were desired—to their audiences. Like these photographs, they were rooted in the ordinary and the commonplace, and derived from them their energy and freedom from temporal aims, as do most works which have a vitality that is not synthetic, factitious, or exterior to them.

But objectivity is not enough without other gifts to complement it, and the realism of the ordinary cannot become memorable without the attributes of evocation and suggestion. Perception, discrimination, and personal style are all necessary for the transformation of the commonplace: anybody's snapshots are what you have without them. This transformation, eminently possible with the camera and one of the richest traits of its genius, is admirably effected here. It makes valid the position of photography among other arts, despite the media snobbery of art historians (who could not carry on without the utilities of photographic reproduction), and of many arrogant and thoughtless people who are as reprehensible as those photographers who refuse to accept anything which has preceded them or has not proceeded from their medium. The reiterations of the media-conscious recall Zola's statement: *A work of art is a detail of nature seen through a temperament.*

It may be a painting, sculpture, wood-cut, engraving, etching, lithograph, or photograph; for notwithstanding a catchy and gadgety saying which has stopped dead many an argument in the last few years, the medium is no more important than any of the other essential elements which must work together in equilibrium to bring to permanence the elusive and ineffable. Natali has used his medium unpretentiously and surely, and the photographic quality of these pictures is so obvious it needs little comment. They are aided by a technique so accomplished it may be compared to a system of good manners which has become natural, easy, and almost unnoticeable. Even the processes of selection and design take their place in an ensemble where the object is not dissonance to attract attention, but a harmony susceptible to adaptability and variation; and never is there that concentrated practice of design which has shackled some photographers with a tyranny that excludes almost everything but itself.

In the photographs in the book before you these characteristics have been brought to a felicitous balance which has no need for the expedients of the bizarre and esoteric or imitations of avant-garde movements born fifty years ago. As in most good things, there is no attempt at obscurantism by intellectual circumlocution and esthetic exclusiveness, and you do not need a special situation or an oneiric condition to arouse your particular response. Because of all there is to commend them, they elicit much, suggesting the possibilities of the unusual which may be latent in the commonplace, and they should prompt the discovery of rarity wherever experience may lead.

Hugh Edwards

Boy playing basketball

Office workers

Art gallery opening

Office workers after work

Debutante ball

Newsmen at a public demonstration

High school prom

Dancer at a businessmen's party

Young woman in her kitchen

Julie Arvan and Karen Nauta at a party

Greg Podalski in a restaurant

Waitress

Ice cream vendor and customers

Newlywed couple

Ana Kuzich

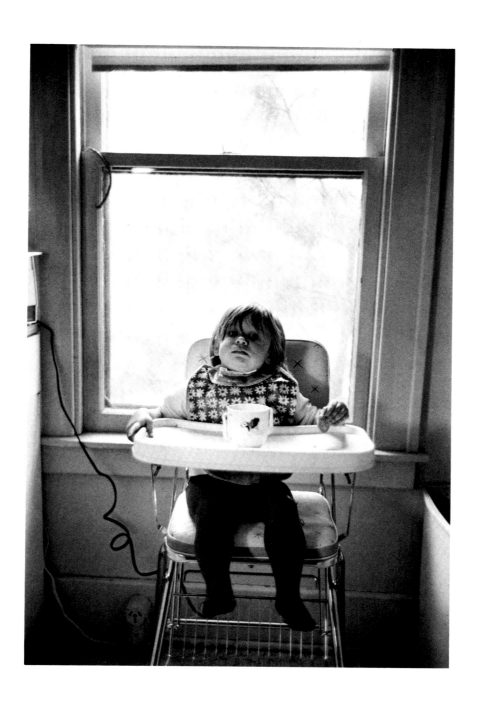

Executives' club luncheon

A family

Couple at a public gathering

High school basketball team practicing

Ushers at a wedding

Mother telephoning

High school students

Robert Surdam, President, National Bank of Detroit

William Day, President, Michigan Bell Telephone Company

Businessman at a press party

Gilbert and Lila Silverman with their children Paul and Eric

Boys on canal bank, springtime

Sunday morning

Auto show

Couple in front of art museum

.

Jim and Judy Yardley with their dogs Sport and Barney

Gas station attendant

Scott and Freddie Turner

Young people, Jefferson Avenue at Conners

Vincenzo Natali, one day old

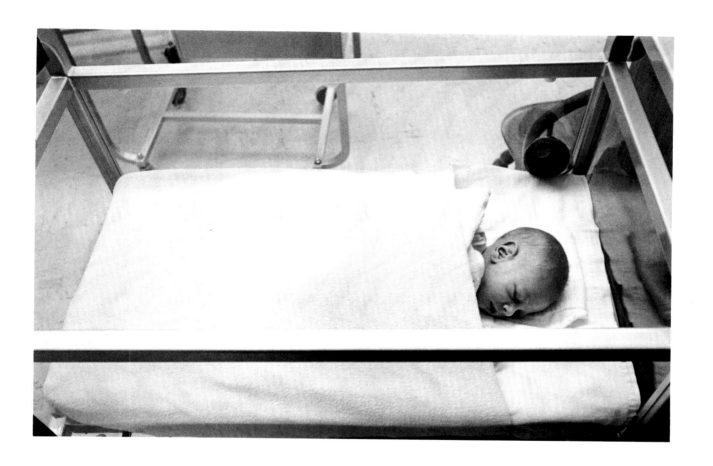

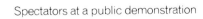
Spectators at a public demonstration

Boy in a neighbor's backyard

Suburban girls shopping downtown

Typesetting shop employee

Executive secretary

Dean Turner with kitten

Margaret Carpenter at home

Ann Davis with her children

Grosse Pointe art show

North Side, shoeshine parlor

Husband and wife with youngest child

Young men, Woodward Avenue

Pool player, eastside pool room

Hair wash and dye room in beauty salon

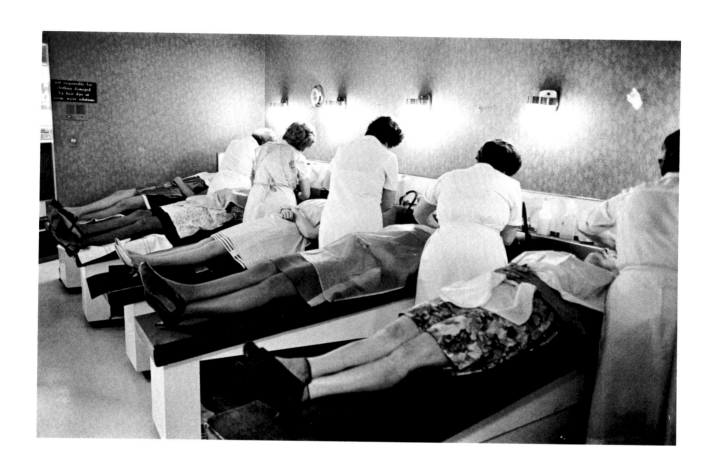

Jerome Cavanaugh, Mayor of Detroit 1962-1970

Friends

Young man, Mack Avenue at Lillibridge

Bolt and nut sorters

Singing period at the Four Freedoms, apartment building for elderly people

Children and soldiers, 1967 Detroit riot

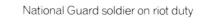

National Guard soldier on riot duty

Incident, Belle Isle

Public protest

First night at the opera

Girls at a municipal beach

Mr. and Mrs. Robert Reid with their grandson Leon

Community Patrol Corps member

High school student

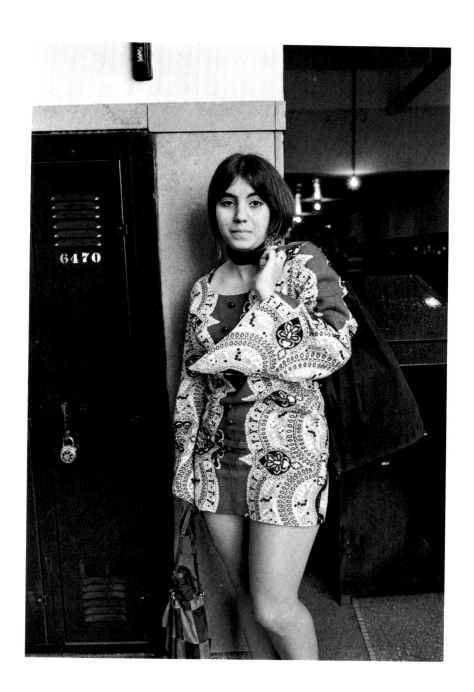

Shriners' convention

Rita Syzdek

Woman painting chair in her backyard

A retired couple

Young woman waiting for bus in front of tire factory

Armed Forces' Day parade spectators

Chronology

1933 August 10, born in Utica, New York.

1938-51 Attended public schools in Carthage, New York.

1951 Entered United States Coast Guard Academy. Became interested in photography; photographed for school newspaper, magazine, and yearbook.

1954 Resigned from Academy. Went to New York City; studied at the School of Modern Photography for short time. Apprenticed to the photographer Anton Bruehl.

1956-58 Drafted into United States Army; served as radio operator in Germany.

1959 Discharged from the Army and back in New York; worked in studio of William Syzdek.

1960 Made series of photographs in New York subway as independent project.

1961 Went to England and on return to the United States worked as reporter-photographer for a newspaper in Watertown, New York. Married Gale Davis. Recalled to Army during Berlin crisis.

1962 Stationed at Ayer, Massachusetts; did series of photographs of houses. Transferred to Ozark, Alabama, and discharged from Army. Went to New Orleans and worked part time for an industrial photographer, beginning New Orleans series of photographs.

1963 Moved to Chicago; worked part time for Ebony Magazine and as free-lance photographer; did Chicago series of photographs.

1964 Moved to Watertown, New York; opened photography studio; made series of photographs of Watertown and surrounding area.

1966 Moved to Detroit and worked for one year in advertising studio, then as free-lance photographer; started Detroit pictures.

1967 During convalescence after riding accident in Arizona reviewed his complete work and discovered the orientation it had taken.

1970 Completed Detroit photographs. From September 1970 until May 1971, Visiting Associate Professor of Photography at the School of The Art Institute of Chicago.

1971 Awarded John Simon Guggenheim Memorial Fellowship.

The following is a partial listing of exhibitions, published photographs and collections.

One-Man Exhibitions

1969 "New American People," The Art Institute of Chicago

Photography/Cinematography Gallery, Roxbury, Massachusetts

ITEK Gallery, Lexington, Massachusetts

1970 School of the Art Institute of Chicago

Galeria Neri Zagal, Peterborough, New Hampshire

1971 School of the Art Institute of Chicago

Group Exhibitions

1961 Image Gallery, New York City (with Rosalie Vogel)

1962 Karen Horney Foundation, New York City

1963 "Photography '63," New York State Exposition, Syracuse and the George Eastman House, Rochester, New York

1964 "Contemporary Photographs from the George Eastman House Collection, 1900-1964," New York World's Fair and George Eastman House

1965 "Two Photographers," George Eastman House (with Oscar Bailey)

1966 "American Photography: The Sixties," Sheldon Memorial Art Gallery, University of Nebraska, Lincoln, Nebraska

1967 "The City: A Photographic Essay," Rockford College, Rockford, Illinois

"Contemporary Photography since 1950," a traveling exhibition circulated by the New York State Council on the Arts, prepared by the George Eastman House

"Photography in the Twentieth Century," a traveling exhibition prepared by the George Eastman House in collaboration with the National Gallery of Canada, Ottawa

1968 "Young Photographers '68," Department of Creative Arts, Purdue University, Lafayette, Indiana

1970 "Metropolitan Middle Class," Creative Photography Gallery, Massachusetts Institute of Technology, Cambridge, Massachusetts.

"Social Science and Modern Photography," Princeton University School of Architecture, Princeton, New Jersey.

Photographs in Published Sources

American Photography: The Sixties.
University of Nebraska, Lincoln, 1966.
One photograph, p. 30.

Modern Photography Annual '71.
Billboard Publications, Inc., New
York, 1970. One photograph, p. 96.

Newhall, Beaumont, "Reality/USA,"
Art in America, 52:6 (1964). One
photograph, p. 91.

Photography Annual 1961. Ziff-Davis
Publishing Co., New York, 1960.
One photograph, pp. 146-147.

*Photography in the Twentieth
Century.* Horizon Press, New York,
1967. One photograph, p. 126.

Photography '63. George Eastman
House, Rochester, 1963. One photograph, p. 58.

U.S. Camera World Annual 1970.
U.S. Camera Publishing Corp., New
York, 1969. Four photographs, p. 133.

Photographs in Museum Collections

Museum of Modern Art,
New York City

The Art Institute of Chicago

George Eastman House, Rochester